The Date Fruit Elegies

Bilingual Press/Editorial Bilingüe
Canto Cosas

Series Editor
Francisco Aragón

Publisher
Gary D. Keller

Executive Editor
Karen S. Van Hooft

Associate Editors
Adriana M. Brady
Brian Ellis Cassity
Amy K. Phillips
Linda K. St. George

Address:
Bilingual Press
Hispanic Research Center
Arizona State University
PO Box 875303
Tempe, Arizona 85287-5303
(480) 965-3867

For Francisco —

The Date Fruit
Elegies

Poems by
John Olivares Espinoza

Bilingual Press/Editorial Bilingüe
Tempe, Arizona

NHM
2011

Library of Congress Cataloging-in-Publication Data

Olivares Espinoza, John.
  The date fruit elegies / John Olivares Espinoza.
    p. cm.
  ISBN-13: 978-1-931010-51-1 (alk. paper)
  ISBN-10: 1-931010-51-X (alk. paper)
  I. Title.

  PS3565.L4565D38 2008
  811.54—dc22   2008017159

PRINTED IN THE UNITED STATES OF AMERICA

Front cover art: from the Lotería Series *(2005–2007) by Gene Flores*

Cover and interior design by Bill Greaves

This publication is supported by the Arizona Commission on the Arts with funding from the State of Arizona and the National Endowment for the Arts.

Arizona
Commission
on the Arts

NATIONAL
ENDOWMENT
FOR THE ARTS

Source acknowledgments are on p. 77.

Canto Cosas

Funded in part by grants from the National Endowment for the Arts and the Arizona Commission on the Arts, this new series is designed to give further exposure to Latina and Latino poets who have achieved a significant level of critical recognition through individual chapbooks and publication in periodicals or anthologies or both, but who have not necessarily had their own books of poetry published. Under the watchful eye of series editor, poet, and small press publisher Francisco Aragón, the books in Canto Cosas aim to reflect the aesthetic diversity in American poetry. There are no restrictions on ethnicity, nationality, philosophy, ideology, or language; we will simply continue our commitment to producing high-quality poetry. The books in this series will also feature introductions by more established voices in the field.

For my mother, Socorro. For my father, Manuel.
And for my brothers, Luis and Albert.

. . . You've never
done something so simple, so obvious,
not because you're too young or too dumb,
not because you're jealous or even mean
or incapable of crying in
the presence of another man, no,
just because you don't know what work is.

—Phillip Levine, *What Work Is*

Contents

Twenty-Five-Cent Stories: Please Insert Coin(s)

Gardeners Of Eden

Acknowledgments

This book would not be in existence if it were not for Francisco Aragón, Gary Keller, Karen Van Hooft, and the entire staff at Bilingual Press. Much gratitude to you all.

Thanks to the editorial staff at Swan Scythe Press for choosing *Aluminum Times* as the first-place winner for their 2001 Poetry Chapbook Contest. Thanks to *El Andar* for choosing "CA Redemption" as the first-place winner in the *El Andar* Prize for Literary Excellence in Poetry.

At the National Book Foundation Summer Writing Camp, I have Meg Kearney to thank for allowing me to spend a few weeks at Bennington College with the likes of the wonderful writers-in-residence and down-to-earth writer-counselors. And to Henry Leung and Muska Nassery—you two are next.

Many thanks to Sandra Cisneros and the wonderful community support I received at the Macondo Writers' Workshop in San Antonio, Texas. Gracias to the support staff and the hundred-plus Macondistas, in particular Cecilia Ballí, Alex Espinoza, Diana Marie Delgado, Richard Blanco, Ruth Behar, and Fan Wu.

I give my gratitude to my mentors, friends, and allies who have selflessly invested themselves in seeing that this book reaps the harvest of success by offering suggestions, guidance, and encouragement: Christopher Buckley—mentor to me and a lot like me out there—and my teachers at the University of California, Riverside. At Arizona State University, I'd like to thank Alberto Ríos, Karla Elling, Jeannine Savard, Beckian Fritz Goldberg, Norman Dubie, and Dr. Manuel de Jesús Hernández-Gutiérrez. I would also like to acknowledge my MFA cohorts, in particular KGW, BCN, KFC, JR, and of course, MAC.

Embracing thanks to Rigoberto González, Eduardo C. Corral, Gary Soto, Rich Yáñez, CLICA and *Con Tinta,* Stuart Bernstein, Sandra McPherson, and Diana Rendón.

This book was written with financial help from the Elizabeth George Foundation.

Research for this book was supported in part by a grant from the Paul and Daisy Soros Fellowship for New Americans. There I would like to acknowledge the support and encouragement from Warren Ilchman and Carmel Geraghty. The program is not responsible for the views expressed.

Acknowledgment pages tend to be long when you've been working on a book since you were twenty years old.

How can I forget to thank Joshua Paredes and Mario and Denise Anima, who all helped keep this poet afloat in my post-MFA purgatory?

And to Mónica—who will have to put up with my writer's quirks from now to the hereafter. Thank you for your support, support, and loving support.

Foreword: Ready for the Work

Christopher Buckley

If you have picked up this book, odds are that you did so to read the poems and not to read a prose introduction—praiseful as it may be—by an older poet. My recommendation is that you do just that: skip this, and go directly to the poems, for they will reward your interest and effort tenfold and say all that truly needs to be said.

That said, I am nonetheless happy to point to the virtues of the poet, these poems, and the book, as I value them enormously and believe they contribute a great deal to our literature and common humanity.

First, a disclaimer. Many years back, as an undergraduate, John Olivares Espinoza was my student. However, the ready facts of his early career—that he very successfully completed a graduate degree, that he won writing grants and chapbook contests, that he has been published in well-known literary journals, that he is making a life as a teacher of writing, and that he now has this exceptional book in the world—are more than enough impartial validation for his talent and accomplishments.

There is nothing easier for a teacher of writing than to walk into a beginning workshop and recognize a natural talent. It happens rarely—the subject and voice presenting themselves clearly from the get-go—and when a really gifted writer appears, the work, even in the earliest drafts, hits you like an electric shock. So in truth, I do not know that I taught John all that much. I did a little "housekeeping" in his early drafts, pointed him in the direction of poets such as Gary Soto, Philip Levine, Larry Levis, Czeslaw Milosz, Gerald Stern, and Mary Oliver. You learn from the best. No secret there. I emphasized revision and the hard work of writing, but John had arrived with a profound work ethic. He also had a habit of paying attention to the world and a desire to bear witness to his life and the lives of others. He was and is a modest man, and his sense of humility enabled him to learn quickly and to give himself wholeheartedly to his subjects. The poet is never more important than the poem—one of the hallmarks of the work in your hand.

For three years at UC Riverside, one of my oldest friends in poetry, Gary Soto, taught with me. I think one of the first books I showed John was *The Elements of San Joaquin*, and then *Where Sparrows Work Hard*. Almost all the lessons John needed in craft, he picked up early on from reading Soto, whose example John was quick to incorporate into his own writing—finding language that was fresh in phrasing and imagery and yet accurate and experiential. John also picked up skills and strategy from writers as far apart as Larry Levis, Tu Fu, and Nazim Hikmet. He learned and valued the deep tradition of poetry as well as the variety of contemporary voices.

Soto was also quick to recognize John's exceptional voice and vision and published *Gardeners of Eden*, a small collection of John's work, as one of the last selections in his long-established Chicano Chapbook series. The old adage that you can teach skills but you cannot teach character is, I believe, absolutely true. And I believe that character, that essential vision in John's poetry, is what first caught Soto's attention, for one of the main focuses of the Chicano Chapbook series was work that spoke to "la vida"—what it meant to grow up and live as a Chicano/Latino in the second half of the twentieth century (and the early twenty-first century) in the United States.

John knows work, as is especially evident in the last section of poems in this book. His was the first generation of the family to attend a university, and he grew up in Indio—that desert-dry landscape of the Coachella Valley with green dots of grass and trees mainly at the resorts and homes of the rich—just an hour east of the "Inland Empire" and further still from Los Angeles. John had worked all his young life with his father and brothers doing gardening. He was ready for the work of writing, ready to take the risk of making a life as a teacher and writer. But it was the lives of his family, of the people who did not stay at the resorts, that became his theme, and his poems risked clarity at every turn to do them justice. John's poems are witness to this life, and with poignancy and inventiveness they reveal the essential dignity and compassion of the people he knows. He values the simple love and generosity of his grandparents and his time with them, yet he is all the while conscious of the greater themes of transience and mortality. His poems are honest and employ a directness of voice a poet doesn't usually command until much later in a career. His poems are emotionally and linguistically accessible, and he transforms the language of experience through music and vivid detail. He is able to write in economical structures that compel us dramatically while at the same time following his imagination—no safe or occluded surfaces for John. I have to go back thirty years to remember a first book this grounded in subject and skill.

The poems before you also display an engaging range of strategies and visions. In addition to the affecting narrative, dramatic, and lyric modes, John offers us a poem of great stylistic ambition with "Network of Bone," in which a distilled imagism couples with firsthand observation of the body and edges those observations with myth and fable and detail from contemporary life. Working in sections, he blends prose poetry with tight staccato lines and offers it all up with a mortal shaking in the blood. There is a section of prose poems in which the narrative economy leads to subtle psychological insights. And there is amazing empathy and cultural wisdom to be found in "Wife and Child Leave Mr. Walton, Spanish Teacher," a persona poem in the voice of a bereft Anglo teacher. John's homage to Hikmet, "Things I Didn't Know I Loved About Southern California," is a tour-de-force in its adaptation of the great Turkish poet's rhetoric and the all-embracing humanity of the theme. This poet knows well more than one note and has written a collection that demonstrates a variety of skills adapted perfectly to the grit and bone-deep intelligence driving his subjects.

However, it is the subject of work—the hard life lived, the small triumphs over poverty and marginalization—that gives this book its profound gravity and raises it far beyond where most first books can even hope to go. To be sure, these poems present a social conscience and consciousness, but the politics uncovered in any of these poems is ultimately a human politics, free of tired rhetoric, cant, and boilerplate, a poetry that is never entangled in reductive ideology. John knows that the concrete experience of a life, specifically and imaginatively rendered, is the stuff of poetry, and that all great themes arise naturally from the evidence presented.

Finally, despite the sense of loss and the life of numbing work, the poems in *The Date Fruit Elegies* rescue the life of the poet and all the people he observes. It is a book of elegies that preserves the culture, history, and hard-won wisdom of its subjects. Ultimately, the generous embrace, the cherishing of life, the great sense of affirmation and triumph over hardship are the project, brilliance, and singular accomplishment of this book.

28

EL NOPAL

This Skin California

"You're not in America now," Hector said. "You're in Califas, the brown state . . . Nobody's going to notice us here."

—Susan Straight, *Highwire Moon*

Foraging

My youngest brother marches
Into our dimly lit family room,
      Complains about the Metro Cinema,
      Where he pushes a broom
Through the tidal surge of popcorn and Milk Duds,
And wipes down the oils of the kernel popper each night.
      He tells me how the chlorinated smell of semen
      From a high school blow job during the matinee
Makes him want to puke, and how he leaves
That task for Carlos, who works the night shift.

      He tells me about his $4.90 an hour,
His supervisor's menthol-breath,
The demanding voice still echoing in his ear.
      He tells me that on his break
      Juan Ortiz, the high school bully,
Called him out because they don't get along
      In math class. He shows me the lump
On his brow, the knot caused by the stealth blow,
      Yet he proudly finished the asshole,
      Taking him out with four of his weakest jabs.
He tells me how he missed dinner because he had to work,
      How management tried to feed the crew
A microwaved ham, and how he was glad
He refused to eat it because it made everyone sick in the gut.

      He looks inside our fridge,
      Complains there's nothing,
Nothing but vanilla pudding sitting on the shelf.
So we drive off at 10 p.m. for a late dinner,
      But nothing's open in Indio, California:
      No McDonald's, Del Taco, or Burger King.
    He swears at the desert night,

As his stomach growls like one of its coyotes.
I tell him nothing's open because it's Thanksgiving night.

>   *I forgot* spills out from his lips. We drive back home,
>   Disappear from the crime lights like ghosts.

Economics at Gemco

My mother pushes a grocery cart,
I tug at her blue pleated skirt.

She puts her change into my hands,
For the old soul slumped against the wall,
His gray mouth covered by a beard of wind and dirt.

I place the coins into his cupped hands
And he stacks two neat columns of cents
Next to his seat on the curb.
He nods his chin half-solemnly.

I turn back to Mother,
Suddenly a cop—he came out of nowhere—
Tells me, *Take the money back.*
I brush the coins
Back into my palms like table crumbs.
As the old man,
Silent as those pennies,
Gets cuffed and hauled off to jail.
I ask Mom why—
We only tried to help.

The cop says bums make thirty bucks a week
Begging for change
And are not too unhappy
When arrested
Since they get food, shelter,
And a hot shower for at least a week.

My mother pushes the grocery cart without a word,
Knowing that as newlyweds she begged outside markets for change
While Dad stole bread and sliced honey-ham inside.

CA Redemption

Tossing out the kitchen trash,
I see a mexicano waist-deep
In the mouth of a Dumpster.

       He's wearing a soccer jersey
       The color of old lettuce leaves,
       His player number is lucky seven,
And maybe his nickname was La Pata,
Maybe he had played with my uncle?

       Now he's ripping plastic grocery bags,
       Sifting through vegetable pudding,
       Used tampons wrapped in toilet paper,
His chinos soaking in the chicken grease,
All this for an aluminum hunt

       The emitted thick aroma of stale cola
       Reminds me of recycling with Mom
       Every other Saturday at Lucky's
       When I was nine: two cans for five cents,
Vending machines that sucked up
And crushed cans into colorful hockey pucks—
Whose turn would it be to press
The blinking redemption button?—
       And watching the nickel and dimes
       Pour a metal rain inside a small slot.

Older, I was embarrassed to rely
On recycling to eat lunch,
       So I left Mom alone
       To empty grocery bags
Full of soda cans, one by one.

Contemporary American Hunger

Mom having quit her job at school
To give her neck a rest, tense from hovering,
Like a desk lamp, over the special-ed kids,
Had made us the newly broke Mexicans
To settle in the Indio of 1986.
Albert and I, barely hip-high
To our mother, unaware of our budget,
Salivated as we thought about the dry buns,
The grade B patties of Argentine beef
At McDonald's—for what our TV eyes
Believed was the best lunch in this town.

To pay for two cheeseburgers, Mom pulled
Out her blue purse, laid out a buck thirty-eight—
Two dull quarters, six dimes, five nickels,
And three Denny's parking lot pennies
Found the day before.
The cashier's forefinger counted the change
As Mom held up the line, waiting red-faced
For these burgers to slide toward her
On a bright plastic tray.

Bun by bread bun, Mom with a plastic knife
Bulldozed the ketchup-mustard-chopped onion
Spread before slicing the burger to give each
Of her sons a half. Satisfied, we went ahead and ventured
Through a rainbow of tubes and hollow balls
With the blond heads whose stomachs were full
Of Big Macs and Happy Meals. But we were happy too—
Better than staying at home on a Saturday eating
Rows of potato tacos after our yard chores.
Did Mom sit there and watch us play?

I only remember her fingers neatly wrapping
The remaining half in the greasy red-and-yellow paper,
Then tucking the lump away in her purse, sustenance for later.

Riding with My Brother to the Dump

I   *Dump Truck*

A white Chevy, the cab burdened
With a week's worth of yard clippings.
My brother Luis races the wind,
Floors it downhill
Spraying grass on the highway—
Gardener's rain.

II   *Clothes*

Flat ball caps laid low.
Old jeans passed down from brothers
To whomever they fit best.
Plastic supermarket sunglasses
Reflect shirtless children
Slipping pebbles in their mouths,
The salty plums of earth.

III   *The Dump*

The truck's hydraulics,
A weightlifter's metal arms
Pressing the cab,
Garbage slides slowly—
Spinach from a can.
Wet clumps stubborn
As confessions to a priest
To broom off.
I slip on the fermentation
We call lawn beer.

IV   *Us Brothers at the Dump*

Hi-tops stomp around
Uncovering plastic army soldiers
Amputated from a backyard ground war,
Barbie dolls headless & stripped.
Dad speaks to an old man
Who sits in a folding chair fanning flies
With a piece of Frosted Flakes box.
We ask, where are those missing heads?

V   *Arriving Home*

We drive away at dusk
To the final segments of *Batman,*
To flat TV dinners,
& more work to do.
Drive away to our silence
Broken by yawns, exhausted
For having been so young
& made to mingle in such a place
Where all good efforts
Settle quietly bowed to the sun,
To become nothing—
Land filled with former desires.

Las cucarachas

Roaches sniff
  with their two
    strands of hair
      around the kitchen
    and slip through
   the cereal box-tops
 as easily as any envelope
 slides beneath a door.
   They munch on dry corn-
     flakes you thought
     were raisin bran.
  In the bathroom,
 they dip their faces
in the uncapped
 toothpaste and massage
   their bellies
     against the bristles
     of your toothbrush.
     At night, they climb
   over the ravine
 of your mouth
while you snore
and become the first
  things you see waking
    from a dream.
     They tickle your toes
    when you put on
  your boots.
 When I turn on
the light before work
  I see them
    on their knees,
     elbows resting

on the roach trap,
pincers pressed
in prayer,
offering thanks
and grace
to a god who favors
them with the lost
harvest of the earth.

Network of Bone

I

No muscle in sight. The sandwich flab
Circles across the navel like Saturn's rings.

Shoulders diving-board narrow.
Hips the width of a cereal box.

As the Greeks to their skies, someone
Once connected the constellation of Hercules
With the moles on my back.

II

Though my arms appear thin enough to shatter midway a set of push-ups,
my biceps are oranges covered in flesh. Darker skin from the elbow down,
it's not a farmer's tan, but a gardener's—after summer months of mowing
and raking in T-shirts from the previous school year, whose tears and
holes have me looking back, holding on to nothing.

III

I've seen men my age whose arms are bigger than my legs.

IV

Even with the grace and speed of Mercury's wings
Donned on my ankles, these feet
Couldn't outrun an arthritic greyhound.

V

I've learned patience through facial imperfections: cheeks scarred by
scratching and the picking of high school zits. My ears stick out like
satellite dishes casting shadows of their own as I walk down a sidewalk
at high noon. My nose—a question mark tracing back to Zapata, who
opposed the state at every turn. Left eye out of focus because of slight
astigmatism blurs the grace of the world, making the orange blossoms of
La Quinta appear like desert snow. Teeth stained yellow with the constant
sips of Coca-Cola, teeth straightened by metal brackets and wires, have
now shifted out of place, like pebbles in Mojave wind. My hair, midnight
waves receding from the shoreline.

VI

My heart beats endlessly behind
This visible network of bone.
My heart pumping evidently that this man
Walking the streets is not a skeleton out of its coffin.

Love Simple

Young love was simple.
A bowl-of-alphabet-soup
Simple. Every morning
At a quarter-to-eight
I strode coolly to summer
School, hair slicked back
As if I were some Valentino
From the black and white
Films. Her name was Spanish
For Juliet. I left home
Early to those tiny braces
That lined her smile like books
On a shelf. She scented her hair
With lemon shampoo, curled
The ends into dark ribbons
Just for me. Once after lunch,
She fed me: bought me a burrito
My few dimes couldn't buy,
And still let me rub the soft
Loaf of her inner thigh
As our classmates' heads
Were craned toward *Gandhi*,
A film about a man I refused
To believe was willingly thinner
Than me. My first kiss
Happened in a public library,
Somewhere between the shelves
Of botany and cardiology,
Though we were sent to research
World War II. Me, I lost the war
Against badly timed involuntary erections.

She was an older and experienced
Woman—By fifteen she had French
Kissed. So I made my first move:
A poorly aimed smooch at the corner
Of her mouth. When she surprised
Me with something slippery and soft,
I pulled away and asked, "Was that
Your tongue?" "As if it could've been
Anything else," she said, wiping
The smoke of lipstick smeared
On my lips. She left me tingling
Inside my mouth and with a tendency
To walk the library all afternoon
Wearing my open-book smile,
My face flushed pink from simple love.

The Day Before Fall on Palo Verde

My brothers and I cool off in the yard
Of our new home with hoses and spray bottles—
Our faces filled with laughter and clear skies.
Two older boys on a motorbike take a spin around the block.
Their middle fingers in the air
Cut through the afternoon like car antennas.
They park their bikes on our front yard
And with reasons only bullies know,
Approach my older brother and say,
"Come here, we want to show you something."
Their walks heavy with boots and meanness.
Frightened, my brother jogs backward
Toward a vacant lot of creosote.
They grin at us like they didn't mean business:
Their teeth gray as curbstones.
The sun yells its loudest before dusk.
The leaves brown like our arms and necks.
The scent of Mom's potatoes swirls with the blackbirds,
Winged witnesses watching us from the phone lines.
Somewhere miles away,
Dad hoses grass clippings off driveways
And leaves a track of wet boot prints
For his tired shadow to follow. Somewhere else,
The first girl I have fallen in love with in that polluted city
Recites the times table in her kitchen, while
Rolling tortilla flour into one imperfect moon after another.
The gap between my molars tastes like saltwater.
As the earthworms belly their way back
Into the pores of mud, the world darkens.
Who will save my brother?

Mother, a kitchen knife in her hand,
Waves away the boys off the yard.
The blade and its broad reflection
Are enough to drink the last summer day of 1986
And all its sunlight with a great metallic thirst.

13

LA MUERTE

The Date Fruit Elegies

Dedicated to the memory of Roxana Rivera

Slower than the Days of My Grandfather

The backseat of the Cougar.
Driving back from Limón's Food Market.
My brothers are reading comics,
Their minds wandering Gotham City.
I look up at my abuelito.
His head small, round,
Wrinkled like a roasted walnut.
The scent of Old Spice
On his coconut-shell cheeks.
Doritos on my breath,
Budweiser on his.
I ask him in Spanish
Who gave him his plaid shirt.
Tu mamá, de la K-mar'.
I offer him a sip
Of my strawberry Slush Puppie,
Thank him for the candy,
And close my eyes.

*   *   *

Winter Saturday morning.
Driving back from Riverside
To Las Palmas Funeral Home
I watch the date palms
Pass slower than the days
Of my grandfather.
I walk inside the chapel
And spot a coffin, a corpse,
Displayed in the open.

I look down at my abuelito,
His face stretched like putty,
His cheeks cold
As the slushies of my childhood.
Tía Lola closes his casket.
Driving off into
The long stretch of gray highway
Toward the burial waiting ahead,
I watch the date palms
Pass like pages
Of a Bible
Out in the wind.

One Headlight and a Windshield Mosaic

Where's your eyeball?
She asks, pointing to my car's
    Darkened headlight.
        I must've been winking
    At other motorists
For who knows how long?
        The one working light
    Seems to be staring
At my knees, reminding me
Of a song titled *One Headlight,*
    A hit when I was dating
My first college girl.

I remember her nodding
    To that tune as we parked
Behind the Phys-Ed building,
        Our palms wetter
        Than our tongues.
    It was the second night
Of spring. A mute rain dropped
        Before us like fruit.
    Her neck craned toward
The windshield as if looking
        For that one point
    Where the cloud became
    The water, and she said,
        My father crashed
            Into the ocean.
    I'm remembering now her dark
Varsity sweater, her name printed
        Just above her heart.

This reminds me of a similar
    Sweater worn by an older
      Kid in junior high
  As I huddled alone
With my hands under my pits,
    Laughing along unnoticed
    With his friends.
All our laughter joining the same
    Cloud above the bus stop
    And going nowhere.
        Soon, in high school,
His face would make a mosaic
    Of broken windshield,
        Blood, and teeth,
As he made a simple right turn
And slammed into what he
Believed was a motorcycle
He was passing, because it had
    Only one headlight.

  I look at my hand
    Bright from the one
Good light, turn to her
And say, *I gotta get that fixed.*
    It's late and the stars
   Will burn out by morning,
   No matter how sure I am
That they're still there
    On the other side,
Glowing inside the mouth of God.

Watering the Black Pots in the Fall

The pots are endless.
Unorganized row after row.
Black pots, little pots,
Fat ones, small ones.
Dirty, scuffed, cracked.
I have to water them all,

Even the empty ones.
The pots hold infant trees, bug-eaten shrubs,
Violets, petunias, begonias, and flowers I don't recognize at all.
My father can tell me their names.
But he speaks, these days it seems, only to the wind.

Hidden under his straw hat,
His upper lip covered by a Zapata mustache,
He has me out here watering
In the bitter desert evenings,
Because I forgot to do it earlier
Before he came back from work.
How else are you going to learn
Some responsibility? He says.
My backyard is a minimum-security prison
With seven feet of concrete wall.
A ward of black tubs of plastic bother.

There are more pots under the grapefruit tree.
I slip in the mud or bump my head on a branch.
I step on the rotten fruit, ruin my new shoes.
The hose leaks as I stand here
Daydreaming about Anna Estupiñán,
Her eyes that never find mine staring from the back of class.
The cold water mixes with a thick desert breeze
Giving me shivers for the rest of the night.

The chore takes forty minutes,
But I make it twenty.
And soon enough, the next semester will come
With David Martínez pounding Terence Crawford
Because his face is black,
Six gangsters from Penn West
Kicking José Echevera in the ribs,
Because he is from the North Side.
All before completing my freshman year.

How I want to move out
And never be told what chores to do,
Never have to duck another punch.
Never have to hear the slow hum of water
Escaping the hose as I water the last pot
Next to the cherub statue,
Droplets trickling down his legs.

Black Hair Lying on a White Pillow

I am fourteen and I am dead.
My body lies on its side
     As if napping during twilight.

     I am fourteen and this is the year
I was most likely to have killed myself.
     Self-esteem low
          As water running down a sidewalk.
     Ridiculed for my skinniness.
Skinny because I could not help
If a hot lunch was always a buck more
          Than what I could afford.

I would have probably taken a mouthful
Of sleeping pills
          Like a bunch of shelled sunflower seeds,
Rather than using a gun, mostly it leaves a mess—
A bloody diarrhea on a bedroom wall for someone else to wipe up.
Or if I had carved my initials
          Into my wrists,
The blood would have frightened me
     Into calling 9-1-1.
Even if I couldn't use my fingers to dial,
I would have tried with
     My nose,
          My tongue,
               Or even my earlobe,
Only to reach, no doubt, a busy signal.

It would be after dinner.
After Dad came home from work,
Yelling at us like a coach
     For not watering the pots.

After squeezing the clusters of blemishes
Like raspberries in front of the bathroom mirror.
After asking Alisa Huerta for a date and her
            Not even acknowledging I asked.

It would be a Thursday.
Friday would be too late to ask for a date.
And that following Friday
            I would be in the *Desert Sun*,
Somewhere after the front page, but before *Family Circus*.
And I would be
            The center of attention
                        In high school for once.
Before I'm forgotten over the weekend. I would be remembered
            At a half-time memorial:
Football players holding their helmets over their hearts,
Cheerleaders holding my freshman photo over theirs—
            Finally my face between their cleavage.

At my funeral
My grandmother would weep.
My grandfather, stricken with Alzheimer's,
Would believe he was dead
            And had forgotten to crawl back into the coffin.

My epitaph would read:
Here lies John Olivares Espinoza (1978–1992):
Born the same year as Superman: The Movie
Was released nationwide, also died the same year
As Superman, once being his hero.
It would say nothing else
                        Because I had done nothing else.

God should send me now, back into time,
To stop me. If I went back I'd bring along photos
To show myself and I'd say,
John, here you are in the future,
With skin as smooth as a table counter.
Here is Dad with arms wrapped around you like a scarf.
Here are the girls you will date:
Cheerleaders, models, prom queens
            The ones you want now.

Then I'd show myself a picture taken with Diana,
Our temples touching together at eye level
At my brother's 18th birthday—my brother
Who would've found me lying in bed, dead
When he was only eleven—
This wonderful girl, I'd tell myself,

Is worth enduring those few more heavy years.
I would show the young John a picture
Of my older brother and me, on my 21st birthday,
With his arm held around my shoulder,
As we held beer in the brotherhood of lost causes.

                    I'd tell him,
You will become a poet.
You are to be published young
In tiny, but illuminating journals.
You are, like doorknobs, to touch many lives.

After listening to myself,
Seeing the photos,
I would not believe any of it—
Because I don't believe it now.
Instead I would sit still as if waiting
For mute clouds to speak.

But in the meantime,
I'd pour myself a cold soda
Because it is Thursday,
Dad is home from work,
Dinner is ready,
And I have never been so hungry.

The City of Date Fruits and Bullet Wounds

for Alfred and Sam

You're cruising the streets
      Of Indio, it's Friday,
      Late night in the city
Of date fruits and bullet wounds.
You're driving, your best friend
Next to you tugging
      At his seatbelt. Two more
      Are in the backseat:
The one sitting left stares at the neon
Lights of a 7-Eleven as you wait
For a left turn on Highway 111.
The other one sees two cars pull
      Up next to yours.
They've mistaken your best friend
For his older brother,
      Yell out a few *fuck yous*
      And *watcha lookin' ats,*
Strike your car with beer bottles.
Each minute feels as long as a city
Block, not nearly as short as our lives.

                  When you two were seven
                  Or maybe ten, I remember
                  You were skinny as my father's
                  Yard rakes, and you were leaning
                  Under a grapefruit tree.
                  Your plump best-friend doing
                  Pull-ups on a branch,
                  My brother counting them off.
                  You grew up with your friend
                  Together like two grapefruits

On the same stem, the ones we
Peeled in the dusk
Of an October Monday.
What did you both not know
Of each other?
The first whiskers in the sink,
Fingers crawling under a skirt.
My brother always spoke
Of you two, side by side
In a world of mud-dark places
And dusty streets.
These memories spread thin
Like field dust on our shoes
After a shortcut home.
That's where we want
To go, right? But not the homes
Like our houses, but places like where
You bumped into my brother
And me outside the market,
When our grandfather was still breathing
Steadily. You were melting
Hershey's Kisses between your teeth
And cheeks, your legs
Still broomsticks.
It's these places where we dropped
A little bit of our souls
Like loose pennies
From our pockets.

Alfred, stay like you are
        In my first memory:
Not when you're in your car and
        Two boys step out and fire.
        Not when you duck

Under the dashboard knowing glass
Can't stop a bullet any more
       Than a chest bone.
       Fuck it, you say, *I'm hit.*
       You throw yourself over
Your best friend like a blanket
Of flesh, take a few more
       Hits for his life,
Until some homeboys watching
From across the street
Scare off the locos with a few shots
Of their own. Your engine
Bleeds transmission oil.
       Your last breath cold
On your best friend's neck.
I only want the grapefruit
       Peels in the dirt,
       My brother and I
       In the parking lot
After a trip to the candy counter
With grandfather, unwrapping
One piece of chocolate after another.

Left Eye Losing Sight

As the sight in my left eye
Worsens each year,
The other gets sharper.
My right eye
Tells the other,
Do not fret.
I'll watch over you
Like a little brother.

*   *   *

When I shut my right eye
The world loses all detail:
People become traces
Of themselves, souls of what
Once fitted flesh;
Ghosts whose
World I have entered
Without earning my death.

*   *   *

I had an uncle
Who had gone
Completely blind
By the time
He was fifty.
The first and only
Time I met him
I was eleven
And asked,
What do you see
When you're blind?

40

Nothing, he answered.
Do you see black?
He said, *Not even that.*

*   *   *

My grandfather slept with a revolver
                    Under his pillow.
Once, he unloaded it,
            Held the rounds like a set of teeth.
He handed the pistol to my young brother
And he inspected
            Each curve
As if it were a woman's sleeping body.
Before my brother handed me the gun
The barrel glared right at me—
I stared into its one black eye
And flinched.

*   *   *

Shut one eye as you read
Or hear this.
What do you see out of the sealed eye?
Now imagine it in both eyes.
Now do you understand my uncle?

Wife and Child Leave Mr. Walton, Spanish Teacher

I return home from teaching to a front door left ajar.
                    The silence in the house amplifies
The heartbeat from our clock hanging on the wall.
        I find a note on my little girl's bed
                Lying in the hollow of her body's impression.
I do not punch the wall this time,
                But that doesn't make up for anything.

        I eat some dates left on the kitchen counter
After my wife blended a date shake this morning.
    I watch a few minutes of *Brady Bunch* and Telemundo
        Before weeping into my forearms until dusk.

I think if I kill myself
                    I'll sink nonstop to hell—
    But a freshman Spanish class is hell
For a bald, white male
                Tall as a doorway,
        Pale as a glass of milk.
                The Mexican students mock my accent,
Challenge my knowledge of their culture
    With their quizzes on pop stars and folklore,
        Though they've never watched a Cantinflas film.
And he was greater than Charlie Chaplin.

                My father taught me to tie
A noose to anchor our boat on the deck at a small lake in Ohio.
        I remember his hands—knuckles like ball bearings
    Under his skin, his fingers fly paper-yellow from tobacco.
Thick nails like teeth on his fingertips. No matter his quick temper,
                    We would not have abandoned him.

In a Super 8 motel room across the desert
            She is probably lying next to my wife,
My little one confused, biting
            Into the ear of her pillow, reciting
An Our Father in Spanish.

Before I swing like broken legs on a piñata above the garage floor,
            I search her drawers for mementos.
I find two bobby pins, a busted rubber band,
And a severed blond head of a Barbie doll
                        Which I stick inside my front pocket.
            I search the garage closet for the step
                        Stool with uneven legs.
Death smells of rags soaked in acetone and dry lawn mower grass.
            ¡Adiós, pinche mundo!

      I place two dates in my mouth
            To take with me something sweet.

18

LA RANA

Twenty-Five-Cent Stories:
Please Insert Coin(s)

The Story My Grandfather Told My Mother a Few Months Before His Death

Anoche, I fled this place of horrors. These viejos moaning for painkillers, they make me, they make me tire of them. I was fed up of its janitor's stink. To save the strength in my legs I slept for three days. The swelling in my feet deflated. The clock read half past twelve. I wore my paper gown without zapatos and walked along the highway's shoulder and stepped on every piedra. I stepped on bottle caps. I stepped on broken glass . . .

And you didn't come across any coyotes out in the desert?

I flung rocks at two or three. Bared my teeth and gums. Growled. Los coyotes weren't the problem, though. The cars were. They drive faster en la noche, afraid of espíritus walking in the dark. I struggled against the cars' air resistance, but lost my balance and tumbled on the shoulder with the styrofoam cups. Before my body came to a stop, another car passed through and I rolled again. Then raced one car after another, until I picked up wind and was somersaulting with the plastic bags. I hovered over an onion field and remembered I knew how to fly as a boy. Nightly, I flew over the fields to pick the next day's crops so there would be less work waiting. Below me, El Rancho Viejo, and I remembered how to land: one knee comes out, point the other leg down.

Did you fly through the chimney?

Why didn't I think about that? When I arrived at el rancho, I was too weak to unhook the chain and let myself in. And after all that trouble. I rested on a rock, doodled self-portraits in the dirt for every decade of my life, until I got my strength. I walked back to the nursing home and stepped on sticks of dried mesquite. I sneaked into bed without being missed. When I woke up you were here.

Maybe it was a dream, Apá? It sounds like a dream.

It was no sueño. Check the bottoms of my feet for thorns. Check and pull them out.

Tips from the Oedipal

I'm in the waiting lobby of a Bank of America; my leg has already fallen asleep. A thin woman older than my mother walks in wearing her jogging suit. A man in his mid-thirties, who I think is her son, walks in behind her and takes a seat next to me. He wears his shades indoors and stinks like an auto shop. Eyeing the other customers as they leave the bank, he tells me he's gotta make sure no one makes a move on his old lady. I say I know what he means. Then he tells me to check out his old lady. They just had a baby. She's his wife. I cough. He asks me to guess how she's in such great shape. Then tells me how.

He made her jog to the Ritz-Carlton and back each morning after her pregnancy. Says her body is clear of the roadmaps of stretch marks. Every night he rubbed her down with a homemade coconut oil concoction. He calls this "afterplay."

Have you ever had fresh milk from a mother's breasts? He asks me. *Not lately,* I say. Says he was watching his son enjoying breast-feeding from his mother. So he was curious and asked for permission to suckle. He demonstrates. He puts his two hands in the air in front of him to form a breast. He begins licking at the air-tit. I look around to see if anyone else is watching. He even wipes his chin. He asks me if I knew breast milk had blue tones in it. I think a blue closer to what? The sky? The ocean? A petunia? It takes someone like him for me to see nothing much around us is naturally blue. All I wanted was a bank account.

His wife walks up to him, squeezes his hand before he links his arm with hers, just like a child about to be taken out for ice cream.

Mrs. Flores's Oranges

It's Friday. A slow dusk after school. Anna enters my backyard when she
notices me watering the pots. I shut off the faucet. My hands, wet and
cold—fingers stiff as jerky. We talk of geometry, Beowulf, and flavored
sodas. Anna is the only Mexican at school with red hair. Red as the
shades of autumn. Freckles ember about her face. She wants an orange
from Mrs. Flores's tree. Its branches eavesdrop over the wall. Setting my
father's ladder by the wall, she climbs as I stare at her behind, plump as a
pumpkin. She takes about four oranges in her hand and gives them two
squeezes each. I feel every one. We hide under the blossoming grapefruit.
She pulls out a folding knife as wide as two fingers that her father gave
to her as protection from our streets. She says orange juice is good for the
skin and slices the orange in half. Anna walks up to me and, vampire-like,
tilts my head, squeezing the orange over my neck. The juice disappears
into my shirt. She unbuttons her blouse halfway, throws her collar over
her onion-white shoulder and squeezes some juice over her own neck. The
pale orange strand of fluid running into her shirt tickles her, so she asks
me if I'm going to let it run and let it stain her blouse. I pluck a grapefruit
leaf and sweep it off. She buttons back her blouse. We finish our halves
with talk of P.E., homecoming, and Pac-Man. She leaves, tossing her half
between some pots. I'm left picking the pulp caught between my teeth.

Story of a Man Falling in Love with a Woman Made of Bark

A man falls in love with a lemon tree shaped like a woman. It has a trunk for calves and thighs, hips and waist, the delicate curves of the number eight, and winter buds for breasts. Her arms stretch above to nothing and spread into branches and fruit. He secretly sees the tree every chance he can. He plays her the guitar and sings love ballads in a lustrous voice. Recites "The Song of the White Bee" to her: *You fly with two petals of a lemon blossom / Embedded in your snow fur are the small suns of pollen.* He strums between her thighs and fall asleep there. During windy evenings he dances with her when she can dance back. The man tells the lemon tree how sweet her lemons are with sugar. Twice a week he leaves a hose running at her trunk.

By mid-life, the man's family and friends catch on to his secret. They make jokes in his absence, but by retirement, they accept his unusual love affair. His sister even gives them pruning shears with their initials engraved for their anniversary party. Though the man grows old and sick, the tree changes very little, except for a few new branches as the old ones become brittle and rotten. When the man dies near her trunk on a cool April evening, the tree sheds all her lemons. They bury him close to her. His dissolving bones keep her strong and nourish her seeds. And with a little rain a sapling begins to grow out from an old footprint.

Story of Rainwater Filling the Bathtub

On the second anniversary of his daughter's death, the long dripping awakens him from his nap. It is dark outside. The ceiling leaks and fills the bath with brown water. This makes the man's neck as tense as a fist. Four years after the birth of his daughter, two years after her body was found floating in the bath, he runs out to the courtyard and into a monsoon. There, the ghost of his daughter sits in a puddle, scooping up rainwater as she did before. The puddle boils and sizzles without the presence of flame. The storm beats the man. The daughter feels the dark waterfalls escape from between her fingers. He looks away from her, but the stars sting his eyes.

In that moment his skin leaves the muscle and the muscle leaves the bone. In another apartment, a lonely woman sitting at a dinner table plucks the meat from a drumstick before the man's bones dissolve into rain. He sees what he always took for granted: the purpose of the wind is to carry water where all earth thirsts. If it is too much for the earth to drink, the land will form puddles; for the same reason people store water in containers. The thunder wrings him out from the sponge clouds and he rains on his own roof. He slips into the cracks as thin as the spaces between his own teeth. He drips into his own bathtub and transforms into a man again. It becomes clear to him that rain is the only chance he gets to not only feel the wind, but watch it.

I'm at some Melrose restaurant when I spot him. His face smoothed down from the raging fires of acne. He's wearing a dark suit woven with metallic thread; a maroon tie falls crooked down his torso. The knot is as round as a small plum. A blonde in a blue dress dines with him. A cream napkin is dropped on his table, smeared with lipstick the color of bougainvillea leaves. The blonde in the blue dress excuses herself from the table, insulted by something he's said. He hasn't changed a bit, old Frankie . . .

The Trouble with Frankie Ávila

He remains calm in his chair. I call his name and he looks over his shoulder. When I make eye contact, I call him again. He approaches my table, holds a steak knife to my throat, and asks how I know his name. I tell him I knew him once and say my name twice. He doesn't remember me. I mention the old friends—Tiaga, Boomer, Pérez, and Lomas. I mention the trash-can fires at school, the shattered windshields from the road reflectors he chucked, the drugs inhaled like desperate last breaths; I mention the bullies and their blunt fists he kept away from me; The shopping carts he pushed like a train to nowhere after high school. I mention the armed robbery and how there is nothing to forgive because I'm in no position to judge anything.

He withdraws the knife. He says he can't remember anything as part of his rehabilitation. I tell him I could help him. That no one should grow up in prison. I could teach him how to write; after all this time that's all I've learned how to do. I offer that maybe it will help him make sense of things—those neckties so difficult to knot.

Westbound

The rear tire blows out. Its puncture—the mouth of a swimmer coming up for air. Christmas week. No AAA. No jack to lift my car like a dog raising a leg to piss. No jack to lift my spirit. I wait for a tow truck and it arrives with two Mexican men from Sonora huddled in the back. The truck tows their Ford Bronco, lame as a horse with a broken leg. Inside the cab of the tow truck it is cold and quiet. The heater offers less warmth than my own coughs. I ask the men what they'll do tonight. Sleep inside the car until the shop opens, they say. My car gets hauled to my parents' house in Indio. It didn't occur to me to offer the men shelter and some comforters laid on top of a tiled floor for the night. In bed, I think of the truck driver who pulled over to help before the tow truck. I remember declining his help, afraid maybe he would drag me into the saguaros, thrust a screwdriver in my neck. I think of those men inside the design of the Bronco, bodies undiscovered like the contorted dead. They will count stars through the windshield before dreaming of their wives smoothing the sheets after they've made love, in a town no one knows the name of, where no one stops for a cup of coffee. A town like mine.

Spanglish As Experienced by a Native Speaker

A George Washington quarter was a **cuarta**. Two **cuartas** bought us una **soda** from a vending machine. We asked abuelito for a **cuarta** to play the video game console. No, he said, una peseta. No, una **cuarta**. Una peseta para la **máquina**. He called the console a machine. Like the machine (máquina) that dropped a **cuarta** for every six cans Mother put in. La **máquina** is what Father had us **puchar** across **yardas** on the weekends. At work we ate **lonche**. At school we ate lunch. At home we ate both. **Queki** was served on birthdays. It was bien **gaucho** to have your birthday skipped again. **Skipiar** was done to the unsolvable math problem, which was never attempted again. Half our time was spent on homework, the other half was spent **wacheando** TV. **Wacha** signaled you were about to do something impressive, but foolish, like a bike stunt. ¡**Wáchale**! is what your friends tell you when you nearly plow into them with your bike. A bike is a **baika**. Uncle Jesse peddled a baika to the grocery store to buy leche y **cornflais**. Leche, not tortillas, were heated in the **microgüey**. Un **güey** is a dude. Uncle Beto called more than two people "una bola de **güeyes**." I secretly listened to the Beastie Boys in Uncle Beto's **troka** because I could turn it up full blast. Uncle Jesse peddles back from **Queimar** with two new plaid shirts. Dad's returning from his trip to the **dompe**, where he left last week's garbage. Mother's fixing Spam **sángüiches**. Abuelito pulls from his pocket a peseta, but hands me a **cuarta**.

Story Told While Pruning

His grandfather and mule were coming down a mountain into the valley. His mule carried firewood, an axe, and a jug filled with a sweet rice drink. In the field below was a girl as stunning as a peach sunset. Her red hair was magma flowing down the earth of her back. She was plucking sweet potatoes when he spotted her. Then the mule tripped over a rock as big as a boot. She giggled as he gathered the firewood. He met her at the bottom. To save face, he told the girl, 'Your smile is the daylight spreading like honey over our giving fields.'

That is how I retell the tiny story he told me. *My grandfather had a way with words*, the gardener says. Caught up in pruning and conversation, the gardener snips off the tip of his forefinger. His finger begins dripping like a broken sprinkler. *Would you believe that?* he says. *My hands are so darkened with dirt, I mistake my fingers for rose stems.*

No Weeds, No Work

If there were no weeds, there would be no work, Dad says. He's a machine sliding his hula-hu through the weeds carpeting the rose bed. I lag behind, raking, collecting weeds in dusty mounds until they are too heavy for the rake. My sore hands struggle to drag it another inch. The sun burns my nose, the tips of my ears. It will be hours before we quit and months before returning to the cool air of a classroom, more sleep, and fewer lunches for Mom to pack . . .

I'm raking citrus leaves in my dreams again, even years later. I rake my first pile; toss it into the receptacle, then another one appears. The leaves never stop coming. My mother in shorts appears on her knees, helping me scoop leaves into the can. I tell her, *If there were no fathers, there would be no work*, as if somehow this was her fault. Her knees are scraped and bleeding now. The leaves never stop coming. I clean her wounds but the blood keeps rising.

34

LA ESCALERA

Gardeners of Eden

And a cup was always
Smaller than the thirst.

        —Gary Soto, *Where Sparrows Work Hard*

Grass Isn't Mowed on Weekends

What first comes across our minds
                About the stocky Mexican

Pushing a mower across the lawn
                At 7 a.m. on a Saturday

As the roar of the cutter wakes us?
                Let me take a guess.

Why do they have to come so damn early?
                What do we make of his flannel

Shirt missing buttons at the cuffs,
                Threadbare at the shoulders,

The grass stains around his knees,
                The dirt like roadmaps to nowhere,

Between the wrinkles of his neck?
                Let me take a shot. *Dirty Mexican.*

Would his appearance lead us to believe
                He is a border jumper or wetback

Who hits the bar top with an empty shot glass
                For the twelfth time then goes home

To kick his wife around like fallen grapefruit
                Lying on the ground?

First, the stocky Mexican isn't mowing the lawn
                At 7 a.m. on a Saturday.

He doesn't work weekends anymore ever since
                He lost one-third of his route

To laborers willing to work for next to nothing.
                Second, he knows better than to kneel

On the wet grass because, well, the knees
                Of his pants will become grass-stained

And pants don't grow on trees, even here,
                Close to Palm Springs.

Instead, after 25 years of the same blue collar work,
                Two sons out and one going to college,

Rather than jail, and a small but modest savings
                In case he loses the remaining two-thirds

Of his work—no matter how small and reluctantly
                The checks come in the mail—

My father the stocky gardener believes
                He firmly holds his life

In both his hands like pruning shears,
                Chopping branches and blossoms,

Never looking downward as they fall to his feet
                In pieces like the American dream.

Falling from the Tree of Heaven

I lift my weight's worth of crushed oleander leaves in a can,
Climb the peak of the 8-foot ladder leaning aside the dump truck.

I shake the crush out of the can like cereal out of its box,
Pause, catch a breath of dry air again, watch my brothers below,

My two brothers slowly stacking tree branches on their shoulders.
Father scales a ladder antlike, disappears into the tree. Manuel

Stands spread on two branches above him, trimming away.
The ailanthus boughs, like locks of hair from a gardener's shears,

Tumble to the ground. One knocks Father down—he plummets,
Crashes not on the piles of branches, but slams across a line

Of brick wall knee-high. I should run to him. I can't. We stare
At him lying there, his body bent like the hedge clipper's handle—

Those same clippers, just moments before, he held in his hands
Up in the tree. Father lies stunned on the wall as his back bridges

The walkway. *Can you move? Feel your legs? Wiggle your toes?*
Questions learned from reading comic books,

When Batman's back snapped over an archenemy's knee.
We keep asking questions to keep from hearing the wrong answer,

Because it's him. My father. The blue and black that is not Batman.
Albert calls for Mr. Howard, the owner of the home, who limps out

With a metal cane, an oxygen tank holstered at the hip, tubes running
Through his nose. After a few minutes and half-glasses of whiskey,

Father sits up against the will of his lumbar, latissimus dorsi.
His face shifts from red to white, as if a tomato turned to an onion

Before us. Father gains back his blush, as well as thanks
for his simple life, and has us resume our work. He'll return

In two days, leaving us wondering if his spine is an iron rod,
Or if in heaven, an angel's arm is sore from its catch.

Aching Knees in Palm Springs

One gray Thursday during winter break,
Albert and I plucked patches of grass
From petunia beds wide as swimming pools
Within a condo complex; one-story stucco blocks
For old men who wipe sweat with dollar bills.
We spent our school vacations in shivers:
Raking, trimming, and mowing frosted yards with Dad.
At the eighth hour of kneeling,
The weight on my knees was too much for me.
For each fistful of grass, I stood up to stretch
And let the cold air sneak under my shirt.
When Dad noticed the weeds slowly filling the can,
He turned to me red-faced and said,
You're packing down the dirt, kneel on the lawn
And weed the beds from there. I said,
I am at least entitled to some circulation . . .
I kept the truth from slipping past my chapped lips,
How I didn't care about dirt and weeds
From a bourgeois' garden—these few men
I learned about in sociology class—
Who raked in more hundred-dollar bills
Than I did citrus leaves in a day.
I wanted to tell Dad that these men didn't care
If Mexicans spent ten hours—or even a lifetime
Weeding out the same bed the following week.
To only tell him about the hours I felt wasted,
When we could've rested our sore backs on a bed
And drowned in the lake of a much-deserved sleep,
Or sailed through Tierra del Fuego, us standing
On the deck and never bowing, not even to the sun.
Or how he could have learned to read,
And I would finally show him a poem I wrote.
But I didn't. Because I knew what he would say—

It's the only way to put you through school—this oily sweat.
I kept my tongue hidden behind my teeth
And watched my brother hunched over, tossing weeds
And years inside a green plastic can without a word.

Ode to the Sandwich: An Anti-Ode

Sandwiches are the suitcases of meals:
Five food groups compact, health
And nutrition fit into our hands
Like a vitamin Bible: In the beginning
Was manna, then cold cuts, vegetables, and dairy . . .
No spoons or forks, nothing to wash afterward—

Maybe a few crumbs to brush off the plate
Like excuses for the wind. Without the sandwich
No one would have invented the potato chip.
Or its American cousin in a leisure suit,
The hamburger—the warmer version of its ingenuity.
What about its impoverished relative, the hot dog,

Who brought us use of useless animal
By-products? Sandwiches boosted our economy.
We have created Oscar Mayer, Frito Lay,
Wonder Bread, Ziploc, and the individually
Wrapped cheese slice, thin as an administrator's
Soul. All employ thousands of Americans

Working hard in front of tanklike machinery,
Just for our sandwich needs. Which leaves me
Wondering if at lunchtime, they settle
In their cell-like break rooms with a ham-and-cheese on rye
Or an unevenly cooked microwavable burrito
In the convenience of five minutes?

*   *   *

We ate where the rich would not see us,
That is why they believed we ran
On the sun's energy: The new affordable
And more efficient solar-powered gardeners.
For our only meal in the ten-hour day,
Mom made each of my brothers and me

Two ham and American cheeses on white
Air-bread. The first sandwiches used to have
The trimmings. But the tomato's juices
Dissolved the bread and by mid-morning,
The Palm Desert sun dried the lettuce
Into the same texture of the grass we'd just mowed.

It was now down to plain ham and cheese,
Thin as two sheets of binder paper. But the cheese
Melted over the ham like a lava of yellow dairy.
Next time Mom placed our lunch in an ice cooler,
But the ice melted like, well, snowballs in the desert,
Soaking our bread into white mud.

After as many attempts as hundred degree summer days,
Mom separately placed all the sandwich parts
In their individual waterproof bags.
Our saliva leaked slowly from our mouths,
Leaked like slightly over-watered pots
As we quivered to assemble our lunch quickly.

For added taste Albert lined his lunchmeat with Fritos—
Every bite, the crunch of gravel under Luis's work boots.
Luis splashed dots of hot sauce on his, appearing
Like the drops of Albert's blood from an afternoon
Nosebleed splattered on the hot cement. He bled
Continuously like the mystical wounds from a saint's stigmata

We had learned about in Sunday school, which seemed
More realistic than getting ahead in life as a gardener.
Father's cold bean and egg burritos were heated
On the dashboard—the gardener's microwave.
Our lunches lasted half an hour. By then,
Our bellies were packed like leaves in a can.

We wished our heads could rest,
Stonelike, sinking deeply on a pillow of roses.
But we knew there was machinery to push,
Energy to convert skin into calluses
And miles' worth of lawns to mow
Before we could quit and calm the hunger again.

These Hands, These Roots

Go on, tell me
My hands look like yours,
Nails clipped, filed, buffed, shined.
They weren't always so.
My hands were

Forged from
Gardening, working so deep
In the soil, they could have been roots.
Fingers splintered by wooden
Rakes and shovels.

Some gardener—
Whose face and name get lost
Like loose coins in my memory's
backseat—told me women
Look at men's hands

For dark half-circles
Between their nails, which give away
Your blue-collar status like a pair of torn jeans.
This no matter how handsome your face.
I knew I had hope,

But what about
Lupe, whose mower chopped
His fingertips instead of blades of grass,
Who then preserved them in an ice chest
Next to some plums?

So I scrub, clip,
And lotion my hands with aloe,
Fearing bachelorhood and Internet dating.
I take pride in my hands now,
But what about when

The skin gathers at the knuckle,
And arthritis tangles my fingers for
Cracking my knuckles since I was ten?
But until then, hold my hand
Tightly with yours

As my other hand
Wipes the sweat from my brow
Under the perspiration of work and love
And the fact I know no other way
To wrestle out a life for us.

My Father's Ways of Getting His Jobs Done

Father scolds us at home because that's his second job.
> At his first job, he scolds his workers. They seem slow:
>> Hands cramped from too much pruning,
> Thigh and calf muscles feel like egg whites
Pouring down from a puncture in the shell.
The sun drains their energy like a child sucking on flavored ice.
> Father gets paid to yell louder than the machinery.
>> But at his second job, it's strictly on a voluntary basis.

> Then he brought us to work with him and scolded
> Us some more. He just couldn't get enough.
Scolded us for leaning on the rake for support,
>> As leaves rested unraked—each one a wish
> To be stretched across a sofa asleep,
> Dreaming about the weight of teenage breasts
Measured on the scale of our hands.
Scolded us for not knowing the names of tools
> In Spanish, though we didn't know them in English—
>> Each one a mouth chomping on PVC pipes,
>>> Without a word to say to any one of us.
> Father liked his sons to be like his pliers.

> Scolded for asking too many questions at home,
> We hid away in our room with three beds,
Rushed through our homework, played video games—
> The volume hushed like mutterings during deep sleep,
>> So as not to compete with the sounds of passionate
>>> Embraces during my parents' telenovelas.
>> When we stepped out, it was only for a cold drink.
> Barefoot on the tile, we were scolded again
Because walking without slippers

And drinking cold water would get us sick.
>> *Do I have to tell you each and every time?* he'd say.
>> This was his mission statement.

>> No matter how many times I was lectured,
> I don't remember the face.
Just the voice, a knife in the eardrums.
I remember the swollen chest, the shoulders,
>>> Looming over me like mountains,

>> Wearing a green flannel shirt.
> If we talked back, he would've crushed us
Like a beer can under his boot treads.
>> He was the Big Bad Wolf in a sombrero and mustache.

>>> (Memory, 11 years old:
>> The front yard smells of orange blossoms.
We wrestle with Dad: one son is a necklace
>> With his arms flexed, two sons
>>> Hang on as if they're swinging from a branch).

>>> I turn 21, convinced I'm a man myself,
>> Came home from college,
> Found myself taller than my father
And I realized two things:
Perhaps Dad wasn't such a bad guy after all?
> With two degrees at my side,
>> He rebuked the lazy soul out of me.
>>> And he was never big to begin with.
Was it because I hadn't grown yet, I wonder?
> Or because my head always looked downward,
>> Too ashamed to look him in the eye?
>>> He looks up at me now, all smiles
>> *What a fine job I've done with you.*

Things I Didn't Know I Loved About Southern California

After Hikmet

It's 2002 October 21
I'm sitting by the window on a Boeing 737.
Morning is rising
I never knew I liked
Morning rising like an eyelid revealing a bloodshot eye.
I don't like
Morning, Nazim—as it means working the soil:

Summer soil petrified and stubborn;
Winter soil soft and open. Our hands reach
In to dig small holes
To plant geraniums (petals
Like an exposed heart), petunias, violets
And snapdragons, whose mute
Mouths withhold their wisdom.

In December, when the air frosts our armpits,
We stand by the warm engine
Of the work truck. We want nothing more
From life but the engine's
Pathetic heat. We must kneel all day
And dig, our joints stiff as sticks of manzanita.
But we have planted a thousand flowers
                            By day's end
And brought color to the ground—the overcast's envy.
                            I didn't know I loved the soil.

I didn't know I loved the smog.
The summer dissolves
Thick as a Eucharist on my tongue.
Autumn in Riverside. I'm driving down Aberdeen-Inverness

At dusk—the smog
Has turned the sun to a peach, that ripe fruit
Falling slowly behind the world.

At Santa Monica, ocean waves
Breathe out cool air. I didn't know I loved
The ocean. I never used to.
In San Diego, as a child, I waded
In the Pacific. It was dark and dirty, like canal water.
I stand on the shoreline barefooted,
                    The seaweed grabs my ankles,
Inviting me in for a swim.
The sand sinks from underneath my heels. The ocean seems
                Vast, endless like the young man's perspective
                    On his own life.

I didn't know I loved
The ocean until I lived in Arizona. The surf is six hours away
                        From Phoenix
                On the freeway. I've never surfed.
I've seen it done twice before.
I didn't know I loved surfing. I love
The freeways. We ride the backs of these great gray
Snakes. Next time you drive under a freeway, watch it.
                    It will seem to coil
And unwind above you. I didn't know I loved Interstate-10
Going westbound. For one and a half years,
I drove five hours across the desert
To see my girlfriend. I pretended the gearshift
Was her knee.

These airplane seats are no more comfortable
Than a toilet. We are flying over cloud-carpet snow. The winter
Of my eighteenth year was the first time I saw snow. At the Arrowhead
                    Mountains, the snow was icy and gray;
But I loved it. I held the snow in my hands until it was no more.

Then I held some more. From above, I see the desert,
		The valley that blocks out
The ills of the world for me.
I didn't know I loved the mountains.
Sometimes with shrubs
On their complexions, sometimes
Their tops like gray-haired wise men.
I didn't know I loved the towns with small populations,
Like Thermal or Mecca
Or Thousand Palms, where my godparents harvest date fruits
On a ranch. I didn't know I loved date fruits
And how their skins
Tickle my throat. I didn't know I loved
The palm trees, the palm fronds waving
Good-bye, or the yellow desert,
Or the wild sunflowers,
Their seeds brown like the Mexican girls I don't get to love.

I didn't know I loved the Koreans, Indians,
The blacks, the Filipinos, the whites,
The Chinese, the children of the mix—
Southern California's brown and brown-alike.
I love them too.

Morning is fully awake. The man sitting next to me is well dressed,
Groomed. His breath
Smells of sour milk.

Why is it that when you're on a plane, like I am
On a flight from Los Angeles to Phoenix,
That one feels calm in the air?
There isn't much I could do
If the turbine exploded
		And the plane was a flame falling from heaven. On this journey,
		From which I could possibly not return, I was twenty-four and knew
		I loved myself and the everyday geography of small things.

No Matter How Bad

A Saturday of violet clouds outside.
In my fists, two red and blue plastic pegs.
I throw them at the sun with the force of a small sigh,
Arrogant to think that I can stop this spot of fire in the sky,
The sun that seems to pick on only my family.
Or that I can calm this comet threatening
The world's tranquility and Saturday morning cartoons.
The pegs, light as dried bones,
Fall back to earth repelled by the sun's rays.
I do no more than knock a fig off our tree
And a crow begins to pick at its fleshy insides.
I head inside, defeated by solar blindness;
I trip over a garden hoe left out of place
And it slices me between the ankles.
I run, cry to a mother squatting over the toilet,
Then I'm lying in the back seat of our Buick.
The back windshield webbed with water stains.
The sun never loses sight of me, nor forgives
My betrayal, torching me with all its hatred.

At fourteen, I hoe dried weeds from a thirsty earth
And curse my father for making me do it.
The sun curses him also. After thirty-five years of gardening,
He dies of skin cancer, a dark mold across his face.
At his wake, I try reading an elegy,
But can't get past the first stanza
Because the wash of grief stings me
Like an eyelash caught in my eye.
I try reading it to Mother years later,
But don't have the lungs for it anymore—
She has gone hard of hearing after all
The yelling from her father and then her husband.
I can do no more than fold it in eighths

And slip it into her robe's pocket,
Let it all be forgotten with the wash.

Turning fifty now, with rheumatism,
Each evening I come home with shoulders
Slumped and weary from mowing lawns.
Despite the searing in my knuckles,
Despite the cave-dark air of my apartment,
I write a few lines, no matter how bad
Or uninspired. It is then that I go back
To eat that fig fallen among the gravel
And taste the moment under what I didn't know
Were the embracing arms of sunlight.

Source Acknowledgments

I extend my gratitude to the editors of these journals for publishing the following poems in their various forms and titles:

Clay Palm Review: "Slower than the Days of My Grandfather" as "Days of My Grandfather"

Danta: A Poetry Journal: "The City of Date Fruits and Bullet Wounds"; "The Trouble with Frankie Ávila"

El Andar: A Latino Magazine for the New Millennium: "CA Redemption"

Heliotrope: "Riding with My Brother to the Dump"

Pachuco Children Hurl Stones: "Falling from the Tree of Heaven"

Poetry International: "Foraging" as "Why I Decided to Stay in School"

Quarterly West: "Grass Isn't Mowed on Weekends"; "Story of a Man Falling in Love with a Woman Made of Bark"; "Story of Rainwater Filling the Bathtub"

Rattle: "Aching Knees in Palm Springs"

Rivendell: "Tips from the Oedipal"

Solo: "Black Hair Lying on a White Pillow"

The U.S. Latino Review: "Contemporary American Hunger"

"Aching Knees in Palm Springs"; "Contemporary American Hunger"; "Economics at Gemco" as "Learning Economics at Gemco"; "Las cucarachas"; "The City of Date Fruits and Bullet Wounds"; "The Story My Grandfather Told My Mother a Few Months Before His Death"; and "Network of Bone" appeared in *The Wind Shifts: New Latino Poetry*, ed. Francisco Aragón (Tucson: University of Arizona Press, 2007).

"Black Hair Lying on a White Pillow" appeared in *Homage to Vallejo*, ed. Christopher Buckley (Santa Cruz: Greenhouse Review Press, 2006).

"My Father's Ways of Getting His Jobs Done" and "Network of Bone" (as "Humble Body") appeared in *How to Be This Man*, ed. Sandra McPherson (Davis: Swan Scythe Press, 2003).

"Foraging" (as "Why I Decided to Stay in School") appeared in *So Luminous the Wildflowers: An Anthology of California Poets*, ed. Paul Suntap (Long Beach: Tebot Bach, 2003).

"Aching Knees in Palm Springs" appeared in *Under the Fifth Sun: Latino Literature from California* (Berkeley: Heyday Books, 2002).

A number of these poems also appeared in the limited-edition chapbooks *Gardeners of Eden,* ed. Gary Soto (Berkeley: Chicano Chapbook Series, 2000), and *Aluminum Times*, ed. Sandra McPherson (Davis: Swan Scythe Press, 2002).

Many of these poems can be found for a limited time at Matt O'Donnell's unique Web site From the Fishouse, an audio archive for emerging poets at www.fishousepoems.org.